CM0079B673

**today, the warm-honey smell
of sawn grain,**

from
'remains of Issui'
by Graham Hartill

## ABOUT 'THE COLLECTIVE'

The Collective was formed in 1990 to promote and publish new poetry. Funds are raised through a series of poetry events held in and around the Abergavenny area. Further support comes from the generosity of fellow writers and vital funding from public bodies including the Arts Council of Wales. If you would like to know more about The Collective then contact;

The Coordinator
The Collective,
Penlanlas Farm,
Llantilio Pertholey,
Y-Fenni,
Gwent, NP7 7HN

# THE COLLECTIVE PRESS

# OF
# SAWN
# GRAIN

Poems 1993 -1996

by

# THE COLLECTIVE WRITERS

# EDITOR'S FOREWORD

These poems have been selected from among the rich mass written and discussed by The Collective Writers during 1993-6. The joy of my task lay not only in finding single pieces but in attempting to recognise, and give a fair glimpse of, the distinctive 'grain' of each poet's work. I believe the true test of any writers' group is whether the work of its members becomes more and more distinct - no dominant style, no mere fashionableness, however polished.

At the fortnightly meetings of The Collective, poems with problems are explicitly welcomed. In discussion, there is no attempt to reach group agreement. And since every member's response is sought in turn, the writer goes away with a wide range of suggestions to choose from. Reservations, likings, possibilities for redrafting are teased out and left dangling for the writer to leave or take.

Most of the poems included here were discussed before I joined The Collective, so that during the selection process I was experiencing them for the first time. But others I recall in early drafts and then in revised form, and it is perhaps these which move me most, witnessing as they do to how the engagement of well-informed readers with the writing process can really help a writer realise her or his intention. This kind of engagement is something which many writers in the past have needed and created for themselves. It must have been a normal part of oral cultures but is often hard to find in a mobile society like ours. Posting poems to distant friends for comment is no substitute for the give and take of discussion, during which writers get a taste of how their texts may be received if published, while commentators who are also writers learn, by the nature of their own reactions, how language works - something which may be easier to digest when illustrated with reference to another writer's text!

Most important of all, perhaps, such personal interaction is an important corrective to the pressure of fashionable [and therefore already out of date] nostrums regarding, let's say, the desirability of 'open' versus 'closed' forms or of 'concrete' rather than 'abstract' language. Rules of thumb for beginners are one thing and may at least help to shatter still older fashions. But finding one's own voice is another matter and can be helped only by readers willing to pay attention to how a poem really resonates 'on the pulses'.

If human beings have a sense of emerging futures, it resides in the whole body and mind, not [certainly not merely] in the cultural layers of our awareness. However modestly we may be prepared to think about our work, as writers or as anything else, we are always inevitably contributors to that process of cultural evolution on which - since we haven't altered biologically since pre-history - the future of human society will largely depend. So imitation is never enough. Individual visions matter, not because any one vision will change everything for good or ill but because these visions, collectively, are what society depends on to evolve. So I have chosen the title Of Sawn Grain to draw attention not only to the individual 'grain' of each writer's work but also to the way the anthology as a whole may be viewed as a cut across the social grain 'in this place at that time'. Believing truth of language to be an infallible indication of genuine imaginative engagement, I have sometimes passed over poems explicitly 'worthy' in one way or another but not poetically among the writer's best. The vision is therefore also partly mine and I must take responsibility for any misrepresentation of individuals or of the group as a whole. But I hope that the variety of this anthology - the glorious lyrical flow, the humour, the asperity, cunning experimentation and well-used conventions, surprising imaginative leaps, even at times a certain pedestrian honesty - will be as great a pleasure to others as they have been to me. After many readings, I am still enjoying and discovering.


ANNE CLUYSENAAR
January 1997

# CONTENTS

* Other publications available by these writers, from The Collective Press.

# OF SAWN GRAIN

Cover design by:

© THE COLLECTIVE WRITERS 1997

A CIP catalogue record for this title is available from the British Library.

ISBN 1 899449 35 3

All rights reserved. No part of this publication may be reproduced, stored in a retrieval system or transmitted at any time or by any means, electronic, mechanical, photocopying or otherwise, without the permission of the copyright holders.

First published 1997 by
THE COLLECTIVE PRESS
Abergavenny, Gwent.

The Publisher acknowledges the financial assistance of the Welsh Arts Council.

Front cover illustration by Jeff Nuttal.

Printed by Redwood Books, Trowbridge.
Printed in Great Britain.

Typeset in Futura by:

SCURR

## DESIRELAND

Spread your moth wing skin
Over the star pulsing sky.

The desert of my hands lies wide.

Above us the arched back of lightning
Fires the black marble of your eye.

We move towards the dry death
A millenium to come.

# THE MAKER

As living wood opens its arms, yields to touch,
a shape is created out of imagining.

Eyes are carved out of a snapshot memory,
their lids cool when night slides down the window.

Lips formed from the budded bloom of leaves
hang still, almost smiling.

The curve of the back displays green life
running in lines down the spine.

Motionless on planted feet,
roots severed forever.

# THE RUBBISH RITUAL

When I was little he let me trace the black dust
                            running in the seams of his skin.
I remember too, listening for his bark of a cough
                                    sounding down the road
as he and his snuffling terrier made for the rubbish dump
                                    on their daiiy walk.
Once there they'd sniffle and wheeze through last week's
                                                debris.


Although his dog still blinks in the sun,
still roots around in the rubbish heaps,
I know that he's back where he began now,
and his shadow sits, biding its time, like always.

## THE STONE

In dark
it seams
to matter

exposed
absorbs the sun
like an open mind

but then my breath
could pare it down
to dust

this bone of earth
we stripped
from muscled soil

this giant
raised by man
to pillar sky.

When we condemn the stones
for the sin of silence
they should not answer

aware existence
without question
has no choice.

# LONG DAYS

fold
into nights
cold enough to tack
          flesh to metal

outside
          the chill factor
          of a quick death
                while here
          rigged red lamps
          glow against  gloom.


          Concrete mellows
under warm yellow straw.


Lambs beyond shiver
return to life
in the blood
heat

deep cold
the inner mouth
returns to language.

JOHN JONES

# BACK TO THE FIRE

More than ice
blown in a blizzard
through the Gospel Pass
    more the Devil's mischief
    skipping fields and sizing drifts
    against the drain gates.

       Out there
       a lamb that wouldn't last
          in here
              logs roared red
      and sleep could come easy
            but for the hard
          sweet grains of winter
    rapping on the northern glass

I judge myself
not for what I am
but what in fact I do
within the contrast of the night
      comrade dog and I move out
        amongst this falling factor
slipping away from an empty house

knowing the shelter of the fields
judging the right spot
    in the inter-feared darkness
            body politic is peeled
from a bank below the hazel stand.

We turn for home
cowl tight against my spine
dog's hair
against its natural lie
        our banners go under.

Back to the fire

the cold cataract eye
                rekindles
on a piss poor bed of straw
restoring warmth
            movement
                    suffering
and knowing
what's been tried
has all been tried before.

# MOVEMENT ON A STILL DAY

Dark crow
    one chain
above the yellow stubble.

        An oarsman
    stroking his way
through the still
        chill air

who calls twice
in baritone
before silent
sliding
beyond the old hedge

its second
contours
the broken ground

        a shadow raptor
        chasing the maker
        into a setting sun.

## THE STAINLESS CHILD
[For Jane B., who found the concept objectionable]

It's not a blinking, Blake-ish innocence
this stainlessness.  It's more the kind of strangeness
that makes your feet uncertain in new shoes.

The first stains are not steps to perdition -
just sad, inevitable interventions,
like the first scratches on anything new.

Think of the patina a chair acquires;
all the character arse-kissed into it
by recognition and unthinking use.

This is a chair.  Bumshelf - back up, knees bend,
squat, sit on it.  That is a child.  Show it
and share with it, shaping its adulthood.

It's not a burdensome virginity
waiting like a tin of good salmon; sacred,
unopened till a special guest arrives.

Rather, a swift succession of first times;
genuine never-to-be-repeated offers
of opportunities to observe something

dragged with the red rags of birth from another place,
a time when you were it, the baby, she -
the stop-frame just before you became Jane.

# REFRAMING THE JOHARI WINDOW

An exercise in perception

If you love me, don't draw me diagrams;
Seeing is not the same as understanding.
Draw me the four-cell matrix if you must
But don't expect me to extract a meaning
Until I have told myself in my own words
Exactly what I think I'm looking at,
Written it down and read it out aloud.

Presenting your axes as glazing bars
Only confuses things. You can't convince me
That you can look through a window and not see
What's on the other side. At it, perhaps,
Or even through it darkly . . . never mind.
Leave me alone with it a little while.

Ah! Joe and Harry had a bungalow
With four square rooms: one kitchen/living room;
Two bed-sits with en-suite facilities;
The other room had never been unlocked
For the duration of their tenancy.

Now, since both Joe and Harry worked from home
They each respected one another's space
And neither went into the other's room;
They met at mealtimes, taking turns to cook
Or treat each other to a takeaway.

[Cont:]

And in that common room, can we assume
That they shared all experience in common
Or saw it from a common point of view?
This is to discount the joeness of Joe
And undervalue Harry's harritude.
This would perpetuate the sorry myth
Of roses being roses being roses
And both men meaning the same thing by "anchovy".

So you and I, together or apart
Are still ourselves.  And the old search goes on
For the supposed half-soul.  Let's make a pact
Never to go into the other room
Because the only truly safe terrain
Is that we both know that we don't know.

# GAY SCIENCE *

There are as many languages as there are people
[Not 'peoples', Editor; it's not that easy]
And words mean only what we believe them to mean.

My poem is an invisible sketch in the space between us
Of what I believe my words mean.  Giving it to you
Hands you *carte blanche* on which to draw
Invisibly what you have understood.

You show me yours;  I show you mine:
It gets neither of us anywhere and yet
We are both the richer for it.

Sometimes I can almost convince myself
That if you boil prose till the thin liquor evaporates
And agitate what's left till the words spin,
What settles-out is poetry.

But instinct tells me it lies at the interface
Between what I know and you believe
And may slip between them without touching.

We are no nearer a definition.
Distillations of the very essence of something.
Short-circuits jumping the gaps between minds.

Synopses; synapses.  Whatever.
You could call it like calling to like
If you like.

* a rendering of "gai saber",
the Provençal name for the art of poetry.

## IN MEMORY OF IERTZY JERSINEK

In the cell
waiting his hearing
my charge

iron door
barred windows
his karma

post Belsen
Auschwitz
or some other

squatting
yet another
wooden bed

of all places
in Wales

"people who work
in prisons"
he said
"spend more time
locked up
than prisoners"

oddly
seeming concerned

I wanted to ask
about all those other places
after all
                    at fourteen
he knew the smell
of burning flesh

lacking courage
I spoke of life in space
he had a book on it
and had me keep it

then
matter of fact
'did I think he'd hang'
 they did it then.

lamely
"perhaps not"

seemed a decent sort
as young as I was

but then
he had taken an axe
and calmly chopped
a watchman's head
to bits.

# CASINO THOUGHTS
USA

sanitised
this greed
a dollar
for eternity

illumined opulence
in a sexless dream
promising fulfilment

a fantasy
of uneven odds
and random chances
reflections of reality

then again
losers
can be winners here

and can't help feeling
specially with all this light
outside of time
a certain sanctity

# TUTANKHAMUN

And you
the golden boy
tomb robbed
of immortality

impossible
entrancing
sensuous
your gilded beauty
iconed in time

gift wrapped
for posterity
and the dream
and the faith
and the hope
and the power
and the majesty
and the resurrection
and the glory
and the decay
of crumbling flesh

a mask
your testament

# FLY ON THE WALL

NIGHT-TIME
Sniffing their bedroom
Children put away
He propped on pillows has sprayed himself
Clean tee-shirt

WE WAIT HER HUSBAND AND I

He reads
She comes
bare legs
face damp
dog smell of wet hair
seeming to hide under it

Casually she turns her back
pulls up her dress
turning inside out from under the hem
Bra back

Two hands
red against white
angled strangely
push and
hook apart

Leaning forward slightly
dropping her shoulders
she slides it down
hangs it on the bedpost
turns
tries not to smile

Wet trickles on her thigh
snaking
invisible furrows
like rain on glass

He holds the book low
She
eases down white pants
and I see

The Web

I dare not move

She
shackled just above the knees
begins to undulate
clockwise
Wonderful aroma

I see in infra red

Heat layers like smoke
I beat to fly in it

She stops
slowly starts the other way

Book drops
Hands reach out
one on each hip
and pull

At last sound of snorting

I begin my buzzing

27.

JANE BLANK

# SCENT

and as the sheets turned there was a figure
Music played
Hair flew   up   pouring
like water

Linen   lifted
Underneath   frail pale arms   raised   twisting
snakes dancing

Air churned   scoured through her head
and clouds ran   over

Shadow   light
Sun   cloud
Dark hair like seaweed
Crack   icy cotton
Slap   balloon and turn
Rows and rows of it thunder in wind

White face   a lamp through branches
Wrestles   down   beating wings

Staggers   drunk
In air   sunlight

and now   the folding
Behind closed doors
in the sudden   dark   silence
of an island
Whilst waves toss the trees

Sharp skin   catches
brushes
folds
smoothes
linen filled with air

28.

## SECRETS

The rain sends children whispering
                    among the beech leaves,
Droplet fingertips inquiring each sprung sprout,
Each split bud spurting twirls of tacky anguish
                    in the baby night.


Oh the creep, nudge, finger-giggle.
Curiosity all pattering,
            padding down the gentle foliate steps.
What news passed back
            along the columns of seething tears?
What playground gossip about suppurating bulbs,
Concerning sulking flouncing frond-flirts?


"We have seen," they simper  -
"Thus and this and sundry other sibilances.
We have pondered,"
            fingerpads tap  - "that here are alleys,
Oceans, ponds of space,
Brushed, kept clear busily by seedlings lisping,
Hastened, harassed by our kissing prints."

## SPLIT

Their wholeness lets its parts drift
                    free  like continents.
The rot floods in, sea-maggots crawling.
She butters toast,  makes tea. "Not indolence
But zipped-up grief.  This rain's appalling."


A world that seemed complete, where petals,
Foliations muzzled one another, cracks.
"I shan't stay here.  No, nothing's settled.
Just the same I don't think I'll be back."


On one hand Asia. Oops. There goes Australia.
The Indies are a litter in the scum.
She starts aromatherapy  -  a failure.
He goes to Leeds to nurse his crazy mum.

# PORTRAIT

Lines glide
Riding the character-thermal
Spun out of crackling hair-line,
          swerving to swivelling jawline
Levelling in to expression.
She turns and she smiles
And she levels back black.


The pour of her head
Face-flesh shed from her skull
              to the tip of her kiss
That wrings out the drab and discards it
Lighting the time.

## SHIFT

The bedroom
still tinged with your aura

fragrance
on my pillow

Outside
sharp air bites
ambition cries

Hollow
walking through grey

merging structures
smell of industry

# STRAWBERRY CRUSH

'He dreams of her soft warmth
but as the drums roll
so do the ears'

He wakes
to claws gently scratching

cuffs and black wrapping
gloating   over his former's demise

She lines her lips
and strikes a bargain

*For Susan Frederick*

33.

PAUL AUSTIN

# FAITH

'Murmurs from a crying distance
the resurrection will be sound'

Here    god's reflections
play the finest strings
and cleave their image

Others   have theirs etched
on tall grey trees

## SCHIZOGENESIS

His was a curious crystal world:
A curveless world of parallels
Straight lines and intersecting planes,
Each close-packed and regular,
Hexagonal, tetragonal,
Cubic, orthorhombic or triclinic.
Shapes of softly rhythmic stillness.

His was a curious crystal world
Of habit and exactitude
With each and every day the same;
Each and every way the same -
Repeated sequences of tasks
Each timed by some internal resonance.
Perfection in and of themselves.

His was a curious crystal world
Which,  in confusion when he met
Those less well-ordered, dislocated
Cleaving all his rigid planes
Leaving perfect millicrystals
Each formed in perfect diminution
Of his perfected former self.

# DESK-TOP PUBLISHING

It was here      long before chips
Were handling sixteen bits
Before    they cracked Enigma
Predating    the Difference Engine -
Babbage 1830  -ish.

I remember a straw-thatched village school
Desks on the Parish   circa 1796:
Under a lid inlaid
With ink and beeswax polish
Penknifed with childish imprecision
The rough initials of an early pupil.
First of an ever-growing list
Which by 1936 had grown quite bold:
We learned that  Joe loves Phyllis Smith
And John Swift's sister's growing tits.
In those days what you saw
Was what you got.  Padded bras
More imagined than real
Liposuction undiscovered.

When I was there    in 1952
We'd scratch our signatures -
Increasing the roll of miscreants -
Within the wood with compasses
Scribble notes
Then pin them underneath
To flash a signal when
We put away our things

More primitive indeed
Than modern WYSIWYG
Slower sometimes too
But surreptitious
And - when spell-checks carried canes -
MUCH MORE FUN.

Enigma          - German  WW2 code machine
Charles Babbage - invented  the  Difference Engine
                  the first mathematical computer.

# STARS

From villages    bright with pelargoniums
you can count stars we have forgotten:
you have few big cities leaking light.
In time no doubt tourists will demand
what you and travellers will never miss:

theme parks to the past;
fast food served
on converted megaliths
and warriors' graves;
Heroes   packaged
in a bun
with mayonnaise;
and synthesised epics
of Brian Boru
drowning the beat
of the ancient bodhran.

They will want a flatter swifter path
to what will be the final wilderness
far west of Skibbereen.   Your firmament
will vanish, swamped by lamps.
And you will forget your martyrs    and your stars.

## NORMAL ?

I'm often asked
"What IS normal?"

Thinking I'm normal,
but knowing
I'm a little different,
I say,

"Normal is when
you know you're different,
but others don't see
that much difference,
so it doesn't worry them."

Abnormal is when
you know you're normal,
but no-one else can see it
except you."

The ironic beauty
of lines like
"I think I'm going mad"
is that as long as you do,
you're probably not.

## LLANFRYNACH
[Rowland Watkins fl. 1635-1664]

Rhydio gwenffrwd
i Lanfrynach
a cherddi
yn ystwyrian
ymhlith y meirwon rhwyfus.

Mae ysbryd bardd
ar hawnt
rhwng yw a maen,
yn eistedd ar y gamfa draw
a chwerthin am ein pennau.

Ni welwn
frain yn frodyr,
nid m gyfarwydd
â rhinweddau'i gwrw bach.

Fording clear-stream
to Llanfrynach
poems
stir
among the restless dead.

Poet's ghost
haunts
the yews and stones,
sits on that stile
and laughs at us.

We cannot see
crows as brothers,
we are not familiar
with the virtues of his
small beer.

# ISAIAH 54:1

[Er cof am Anne Lovatt*]

Rhyw ddoli glwt
o gelain merch,
rhwyg llachar
lle bu gweflau serch

bloeddia gân, anffrwythlon,

bloeddia gân,
gorfoledda
am na fuost fam.

Sheila-na-gig
o gig a gwaed
a'i byw yn frych
rhwng coesau llwyd

bloeddia gân, anffrwythlon,

bloeddia gân,
gorfoledda
am na fuost fam.

[In memory of Anne Lovatt*]

Some rag-doll
corpse of a girl,
a livid rupture
where her love-lips furled

shout and sing,
you barren one,
shout and sing,
rejoice
for never mothering.

A sheila-na-gig
flesh - the dregs
of life in cow-caul
smear between pale legs

shout and sing,
you barren one,
shout and sing,
rejoice
for never mothering.

*Anne Lovatt,15 oed,
a fu farw wrth
geisio esgor yn ddirgel
yng ngardd
Eglwys Granard, Swydd
Longford, Iwerddon.

*Anne Lovatt, aged 15,
who died
trying to give birth in secret
in the garden of
Granard Church,
County Longford.

FRANK OLDING

## COED Y BWNYDD

Gwrthgloddiau pridd
a ffosydd,

rhyw stondrwydd chwith,
heb s n
ond suo'r ffawydd blin
a'r hesg siomedig,

ac oddi tanom,
difaterwch
y mamogion
ar ddolydd araf
eu Harallfyd.

Ninnau'n rhyfedd fud -
cwningen
yn hollti'n hadlewyrchiad
trwy'r distawrwydd.

Earthen dykes
and ditches,

an odd, sad stillness,
no sound
of weary beech
and disappointed sedge,

and beneath us,
the indifference
of ewes
on slow meadows
of their Otherworld.

We are strangely mute -
a rabbit
splits our reflection
through the silence.

## THE SILENCER

It was not the truth...

Medicine's tongue a river
       of eeeeeeeee
      eeeeeee
      Is.


The shshshshshshsh
      of a cut car tyre;

   a footstep
      frighten
         to a tiptoe.


The silence of a butcher's window.

# A STATE OF MYTHOLOGY
[Tides in the affairs of men]      for Peter

There will always be the sea,
absorbed in the capillarity of cloth of continents,
traded by rivers, grabbed by jetties,
bartered for salt:  stories
left in white rings.

Oriental vases surf the mantles
of Asia, Europe, the USA, their brittle life
owing more to destructionless passage
than the potter's creative care.

Yet casualties tidemark estuaries,
wader-turned for hidden food; collected,
rubbed, fashioned to ornaments or beads
to circle a lover's neck.

Your lost-counted-weeks of voyage in sixty-four
turned your ten-shilling-pocket out in Auckland.
Your ship bounced between there
and a full pursed England but you entered
a second life with as little as your first.

Brother, oh brother.
Scant letters, the vinculum of our relationship
stretch over water and land.
A Christmas phone call,
a cassette of your broken voice trying; trying.

Trying to change my remembered fourteen-year face
to the bearded one held photograph-thin
in your hand - impossible
to embrace against a salt-wet cheek.

44.

# A POSTCARD FROM THE BEACH

A silk jellyfish
above the sea
has its prey
shrieking; kicking.

Jet black jets fly.
Undecided gulls float,
flap; argue.

The shore suffers stake claims
and is flanked by beach mats;
fenced with windbreaks.

Wet sand further off,
a motorway of prospectors,
snipped by strident legs.

The peyote-button sun
mescalines the senses.
All a fricassee of ice-cream
and sun-oiled bodies.

## CATARACT - THE UN-SEEING EYE

Dimly, vaguely, with thought-veiled eyes
She sees the forms, familiar, undefined,
That pass before her.

So she saw them,
Forty years ago,
Beside the Mother's Help
With the restless, changing face,
At half past six,
Between lawn tennis and the theatre,
For the duty half-an-hour.
One kiss, one cuddle,
A talk about a day
She had no wish to share
And then to bed.

So she saw them
Twenty years ago.
Still shadowy shapes,
Between Caius College and the country,
On a duty day at home
Each holiday,
While she passed from bridge to concert
With a clothes change in between.

So she sees them now,
As they pay the duty call
For half-an-hour,
Talking of unseen children,
Spouses with changing faces
And, through the thickening mist,
Her worn eyes plead for help,
For just enough
To pay the private fee
And save the stumbling wait
For state-provided bed.

But, well-trained in blindness
By her,
Their eyes
See as little as her own.

ANNI WILTON-JONES

## CURED

Year on dreadful year we watched,
helpless, while he put her down,
year        on        year.

No husband he, who underminded
her confidence relentlessly
as water on a stone, dripping,
dripping on her shrinking self.


When he upped and died we sighed
in sweet relief at her release.
No graveside grief at his burial;
under the dripping trees we watched,
smiling, while she put him down,
deep        deep        down.


Then we said you must go
to a Self-Assertiveness Class,

                    and she said NO.

# BEFORE

Her sister comes to say goodbye.
Tomorrow both will travel abroad; one
southward, one westward. Meanwhile,
they sit at the kitchen table savouring
tea scent from warmed pot, waiting for
water to boil and watching low sunbeams
slide the garden wall, flick falling leaves,
shadow stalking cat, skim pittosporum,
snip passiflora. All at once, kettle shrieks,
Dog barks, collar doves lift off and cat
transmogrifies as sun slips out of sight.
She steeps the tea, pauses, fills the cups.
They smile, each to the other, both
contemplating tomorrow; taxi, motorway,
airport, hurry, hurry, hurry, and all the
while, sipping tea . . . . sipping tea.


## & AFTER

Autumn sun,
long kettle-shadow,
empty room.

RACHEL BALLARD

49.

# HERE'S MEADOWSWEET
## 'TO MERRIE THE HEART'
[for G.W. in hospital]

Hush wife, don't fuss me,
these nostrums are nonsense;

there is nothing more
but to watch for the Boatman,

so leave the door open,
dear wife, when you go.

Then, tomorrow, for my hand,
you shall bring a bright obolus
and pebbles of sardonyx
to rest on my eyes.

# MICHAEL WOODWARD

## THE COMING OF SAINT COLUMBA

Between the white manes
On the waves' backs
A coracle calmly bludgeons the swell,
Carving its thin wake
Towards a hard green place.

The Godspell it bears
Sealed in a cask,
Scribed in his own hand.

Tribesmen point and stare,
Then sprint to tell their elders
Of this tattered speck of sail
Swollen by a fair wind;
Growing bigger,
Trailing a pennant of gulls.

51.

# SPRING

As soon as winter yields,
Print the snow
With your mare's hooves,
And come to me.

I have logs to burn
But I shall be cold
Until I smell woodsmoke
On your cloak.

# LESLIE LAMBTON

## DREAM

I got a sense of you yesterday,
smelt you in my bones again,
dreamt of you in colour, your
paintings scattered and complete
and ready to sell.

I, eager as a butcher
to buy the wonderful,
the miraculous;

delving into the perfect
placing of this
against that.

# THE FIRST WINDOW

Bede's Monastery, Jarrow

The light
that trembles
through my window,
through the silos
of the Tyne
and the dereliction
of all our construction,
is the same light that lay
across your face
at matins.

In the small space
of a day
spent at prayer
you wrought one word
and translated all.

So, many centuries later
I gaze still
through troubled panes
to your early reflections
twisting towards and away
from the turbulant proclamations
of that dull sky and those dull birds
rejoicing
in the grey rafters.

If you had been at the centre
of this city, growing
craned and lighted
and trafficked
by the voice of our obsessions
it would have been better
it would have been much better.

I could have coped with this noise
had it sprung out of silence.

# TESTING THE WATER

I could walk into you
like water
step gently
on your shoes
dipping my toes
into pale flowers
until I dared to dive.

Holding my breath
as if saving it
for another life

while my fingertips
prised open
your shadows

hoping to break off
and wash out
any light
that does not shimmer
green and gold.

## WHEN MY WITS WENT BIRDS-NESTING

[Borrowings from Chinese Literature]

### POEM I

I will move from the upper gallery
and slowly walk past the abstracts
with tears, descend the spiral stairs
past landscape, face, figure and torso
and sit under the plum tree
awaiting your return.

### POEM II

With doors unbarred and windows unshuttered
music blown through the elder enters the atelier
softly, softly, like a quiet lute on the wind.

### POEM III

I arrive at the great river
where grass is lush
trees have abundant fruit
and fresh mountain milk flows.
There is sufficient stone to build
a keep and curtain wall, or
a bridge to the opposite bank.

## BOATING ON THE HAN
## RIVER IN EARLY SPRING *

Where's a good place to go drifting about in boats?
　　At a nook of the Han Jao River, where the goddesses
　　　　　　　　　　　　　　　　used to play?
　　When the snow has melted, the ice is beginning to open
and now the pool at the clear spring is a thousand feet
　　　　　　　　　　　　　　　　　　in depth?


We drain our wine-cups
　　and even the birds and the fish get drunk!
We sing a line or two
　　　　and the women complete the chorus -
　　[they are wave shadows, flowers and smoke,
　　　　　　　　　　　as they shake their hairpins . . . ]
the sunlight gleams from the sand to delight our eyes.


* by MENG HAORAN [689 - 740 AD]
Translated by
GRAHAM HARTILL & WU FU-SHENG

# SPENDING THE NIGHT AT LAI GONG HOUSE WHILE WAITING FOR DING DA WHO
## DOESN'T ARRIVE *

The last of the sunshine burns and dips below Western Peak
   and darkness pours through the valley.
The pine moon generates ice,
      the wind-fountain brims with its crisp and clear music,
   woodsmen shiver, shoulder their axes and turn for home,
      the sparrow shuffles down between misty branches.


And here we wait  -  for Ding Da,
      and the clang of his zither, lonely,
            along the pinewood path.

* by MENG HAORAN  [689 - 740 AD]
  Translated by
  GRAHAM HARTILL & WU FU-SHENG

GRAHAM HARTILL

# REMAINS OF ISSUI  [Patrishow Church, Gwent] *

My ochre is easily dug from the field,
my green from the finch's wing
when Spring is curative.

Lepers,
come.

Come everyone with rotten purse-strings

    - here on the rood-loft
       vine-leaves sprout from the dragon's mouth,

     the dragon sucks
       the leaves and shoots of the vine -

and find a hatful of gold on the hilltop:
stems and roots to boil for colour,
ink from Issui's lamp soot.

Come
to this, the Blue Hole: **

    below the sky the hill,
    below the hill his well;

today, the warm honey smell
     of sawn grain,
a heron,
    perched beyond his cell.

  *

Says Issui
to every leper:

come,

consumptives, paymasters, singers with rotted strings,
to where the ash and the holly break
    from the dead bole of the yew

        - the leper's body:
            clumps of hard red wood in knee and brow

            spurts holly,
                shining ash -

and ask for a fish from the heron's bill.
No traveller leaves unwashed, unfed;
one may kill, another bequeaths
a hatful of gold
        to build a church for Issui
                up the hill.

*

Vine-leaves sprout from the dragon's mouth,
the dragon devours
    the limbs and veins of the vine.

Says Issui:

[Cont:]

My toe may bump the crimson bones of the twisted ewe,
my hair be snagged on fence-wire,
still my finger burns the hole in the blue;

you lepers,
pursers,
hydrophobes,
verbicides,

come
and feel.

Says Issui,
hear:

comes
the singer
goes:

his glee is struck from a fret of black and gold.

*    *    *

\* Tradition claims that a holy man named Issui had a cell nearby, probably in the dingle and near to the holy well still to be seen there. From his cell Issui instructed the people in the Christian Faith and won their affection. We can well imagine their distress when he was murdered by an ungrateful traveller who had received hospitality in his humble cell. Because of his reputation for sanctity and the esteem in which he was held, his cell soon became a place of pilgrimage, and the well which once nourished the saint was thought to have healing properties. In the early 11th century a wealthy continental pilgrim was cured of his leprosy by the water in the well. In gratitude he left a hatful of gold to build a church on the hill above the well and this church was dedicated in the name of Saint Issui.

From the pamphlet
'The Church of Merthyr Issui at Patricio'
by Canon Arthur Reed

\*\* "The Blue Hole": a reputed micro-climate blessing resulting in a blue sky over the area around my home village, when it's drizzly everywhere else - or vice versa.

The Publisher acknowledges the financial assistance of the Welsh Arts Council.